LIVING HIS **LIE**, BUT FOUND THE **TRUTH**

TISHANA MEYERS

Introduction

Have you ever felt like you lost yourself in a relationship and start to question your worth? Self-love seems so explanatory but in the mix of a toxic relationship / friendship we tend to lose ourselves in the mix of it all. Think about a past relationship and how it has impacted your life whether it was good or bad. Everything we go through in life, there is a listen to be learned. As we grow as individuals we mature and what was once okay, isn't anymore. The pain you endure will help shape and mold you. The hard part is having a reality self-check. One would have to ask themselves, Am I giving myself love by tolerating things that that may damage my self-esteem, or does this relationship bring out the best virgin of myself. A lot of times the answer is no, but the gaslight you receive on the other end can make you question yourself. If you're a believer, having faith plays a major role. It's almost like, give your all or go home. Oh, you thought you were the only one. News flash you're not. It's not about gloating or taking pleasure in someone else's pain. It's knowing someone has overcome and seen the victory.

Table of Contents

CHAPTER ONE

Let The Fairy Tale Begin

It was the year of Biggie Smalls's "Hypnotize," when New York was running the rap game. I was young and ready - or so I thought. I was what people call blessed. At the age of 18, I was working for myself and living a big dream that most people fantasize about. I made about one to two thousand dollars a week. Who can ask for anything more? You couldn't tell me anything. I was running after the bag and enjoying life. The girls and I were hanging out every weekend in the city, watching the handsome eye candy that New York had to offer. It was never a dull moment for me, but I wanted a relationship that was more serious and meaningful. I didn't know what I was really looking for, but the New York men my age weren't necessarily looking to be in a serious relationship.

That's where it all began, and I went wrong. When God would eventually show me my worth and develop my strength. My life, as I knew it, would never be the same. This was the beginning of my faith being tested. It was a cold

November evening when I was introduced to a man who sold me a dream. Let's, let the lies begin so you can understand me a little better and see how I turned into the woman I am today.

It was Saturday morning when I was awakened by the sound of the phone ringing. On the other end, it was my good friend Tamia trying to book an appointment. "Hello babe, it's me, Tamia, how are you?"

"Hey, I'm good. What's going on?" I responded.

Tamia went on to say, "Can I book an appointment with you today for a shampoo and style?"

I responded, "Of course, you can. Come in at around 4 pm."

"Ok great, see you soon." I began getting myself prepared for the day. I was working out of my house at this time, so I had to get my station set up and pull out all of my products in order to be ready for my first client. I styled about five clients, and before I knew it, it was 4 pm. I heard the doorbell ringing.

"Who is it?" I called out.

"It's me, Tamia."

"Coming." As Tamia came through the door, she had a big smile lighting up her face. "What's up with that big smile on your face?"

"Oh, nothing really."

"Tamia, spill it." She told me that her boyfriend's friend saw a picture of me and said I was beautiful. I was blushing from ear to ear. I asked, "What does he look like?"

"Girl, I don't even know."

"Oh okay, well, let's start your hair before it gets late." While Tamia was under the dryer, her boyfriend called to see what she was up to.

"Hey babe. What are you doing?" A voice said over the phone.

"Getting this head done," she replied.

"Okay, tell Brooklyn I said hello and that my friend Judas is interested in meeting her."

"Brooklyn, John said hello, and that his friend Judas is interested," Tamia turned to tell me.

"Hey, I'm not too sure about that. Tell him to send a picture. Where is he from?"

"Did you hear her, babe?"

"Yup, I believe, Alabama," the boyfriend responded.

"Oh no, I'm not interested," I laughed out loud, and I continued to finish Tamia's hair while she was talking to John. About 15 minutes later, Tamia passed me the phone and said someone wanted to talk to me. I took a deep breath and said, "Hello?"

All I heard was, "Hello, is this Brooklyn?"

I replied with a soft voice, "Yes."

"I just want to introduce myself and let you know that I find you very beautiful. Can I write and call you sometime?" The man on the phone said.

I didn't know what to say so I responded, "Yes, why not?" What did I have to lose? I was tired of that New York, Timberland-wearing, wife-beater swag that kept calling me. You know what they say - every good girl wants a bad boy.

As I stated before, I wanted to try something new, something different, and oh was he different. He had a way with words. He wowed my socks off. But I was unsure about him. Weeks went by and I started to receive letters from him. The letters were sweet and they moved my heart. He began to grow on me, but I wasn't all the way in.

I received a phone call from Judas one afternoon and he wasn't very happy with me. See, I hadn't really written him back. I'm not big on writing, like he was. He would write me a five-page letter; how do you compete with that? When he called, you could hear the disappointment in his voice.

"Hello Brooklyn, how are you?"

"Hi Judas, I'm well. How about you?"

He replied, "I'm not very well, I feel that you're not into me. I haven't received any letters or anything."

"Well, I'm sorry you feel that way," I responded, "but that's not really true."

"I'm glad to hear that." He sounded a bit less upset already.

"How's your day going?" he asked.

"It's going well." We talked for about an hour about life and his son. By the time we finished the phone call, I realized that his son was very important to him and he joined the military to take better care of him. I said to myself, this is an amazing man. I was impressed by the love he had for his son, and he started to grow on me the more we spoke. We talked for hours and hours, all day. We discussed how he wanted a farm like his uncle. I laughed so hard because I was a city girl and knew nothing about cows and chickens. There are no cows in Brooklyn. I would just entertain the idea. Believe it or not, that's what kept me interested. He was very different and my heart craved more.

As time went on, we grew closer and closer. We couldn't stay away from each other. There wasn't a day that we didn't talk. I was so focused on this fairy-tale love story, that was all I wanted. I didn't give anyone else the chance to win my heart or didn't wave my options. I was head over heels.

Tamia wanted to meet up for lunch and hang out the very next day. I put on my Baker's blue boots with my Tommy Hilfiger outfit, and I was out in the streets. We met up at Kings Plaza Mall for a bite to eat and to go shopping. As we sat and ate, she brought it to my attention that she wanted to go see John, but her mother said she didn't want her to go to Cali by herself. That's when I volunteered to go with her. I wanted to see Judas anyway.

Tamia laughed and asked, "How are things going anyway?"

I told her, "Great. He's amazing!" I was excited about the trip because this was our big meet-up after all these months of us falling asleep on the phone and talking about our future. We were making plans. That was a great feeling.

Fairy tales do come true, but I was confused about whether to pick you. That ruffneck swag is what I wanted. Your soft touch is what kept calling, not knowing what was best. Stick around to find out the rest.

CHAPTER TWO

The Meet-Up

We decided to meet up for the first time after six months of talking and falling hard for each other. It happened to be on April Fool's Day of 1998. Tamia and I met up at the JFK airport for our three-hour flight to California. Upon landing, I began to get very nervous, wondering whether he would like me in person. There he was, waiting for us at baggage claim. He was shorter than I thought but handsome with beautiful eyes. He was smiling ear to ear. It was breathtaking and that alone put a smile on my face. He reached out to hug me and I wasn't very receptive. Let's face it - I wasn't used to that type of affection. Growing up in New York and having Panamanian parents, affection was foreign and weak. I thought I was Mc Lyte, ruffneck got to have a ruffneck. I know, I know, I said I wanted something different, but there I was, opening new doors with old keys. I decided to let my guard down and embrace what was to come. Judas helped me put my bags into the car. The drive to the hotel was quiet. I was trying to figure out what was going through his mind. I could tell that something was bothering him and he wasn't saying what. I could see tears running down his face and that was when he told me that the doctor said he might have leukemia and they would have to do more testing. He was so crushed. I didn't know what to say. I just held him in my arms and told him it was going to be okay. Right there, I decided to make this relationship work. I would be there for him no matter what he had to face. My love for him was strong enough for me to stand by him.

Judas made me feel like I was the most beautiful woman in the world. I can't lie, it was a wonderful feeling, and you better believe I wanted it to continue. I was living in this fairy-tale world in my head. I was willing to take the risk for love. I spent the next five days with Judas exploring the military base and Cali. He showed me a great time and took his time loving me. He even took me to my favorite restaurants. By the time my trip was almost over I was led to believe he wanted this relationship and I was so down for it. He started making plans for the future. We talked about everything from how many kids we wanted to the type of house we were getting. Isn't that every little girl's dream? The beautiful house with the white picket fence. I was already fantasizing about what the relationship was going to be. I guess I grew up watching too much Snow White and Cinderella, where they ran away with the prince. The day for me to depart came so quickly. We were dragging our feet because, in my heart, I didn't think we wanted this trip to end.

"Are you okay?" I asked. I can tell he wasn't himself.

He responded with, "No, I really don't want you to leave." It was crazy because I felt the same way, but I didn't want him to know. I guess it was my pride, the reason why I didn't say it back. He packed the car with my belongings and told me that it was time to go to the airport. It was a very long and silent ride. He held my hand the whole way there. As we got to the airport, we found ourselves both in tears. Seeing him cry melted my heart. "This man really loves me," I stated to myself. Who would have ever thought we would hit it off like this? We kissed each other and hugged before I boarded the plane. This was just the beginning of what we called love.

Once I boarded, I was looking for my seat and Tamia yelled out, "Over here!" As soon as I sat down she asked me for the tea.

"Where should I start? Just know this: this relationship is heading in the right direction."

"Oh okay boo, I'm very happy for you," Tamia responded. All I could think about on this three-hour flight back home was how wonderful he made me feel. He was so different from the ruffnecks that I was used to. He was emotionally available; at least that's what it seemed like. I knew I wanted something different, and I felt this was what I'd been looking for. We arrived at JFK at 2 pm, and at 2:15 pm I received a call from Judas making sure we made it to New York safely.

"Hello babe, just making sure you're ok and you made it to New York."

"Yes, I did, my love."

Tamia laughed and said, "Really?" The relationship really took a shift. All I could do was laugh. After that trip, we began talking even more all day, every day. We would fall asleep on the phone because we didn't want to get off. Our feelings grew more and more. It was a greater bond we developed - so much so that I couldn't see us apart.

As we met, our souls were inseparable. It was like a puzzle piece that just fit.

Fit to be forever, who would ever know but God? But I was willing and ready to take this journey. Until we meet again, my love; let the journey begin.

CHAPTER THREE

Suddenly Ghosted and Deceived

It was months since we'd seen each other because of the distance, but our bond was even stronger. We had received the great news that his new duty station was going to be Camp Lejeune, North Carolina. This would be great for our relationship. Traveling to North Carolina is easier than traveling to Cali. I was looking forward to seeing him more often. It was moving day, and Judas was going to see his family and son before checking in. He hadn't seen his family in a while, and he was so exhilarated. As he traveled to Tennessee, he called me every hour on the dot. He asked if I could go see him when he returned. I told him there was nothing I'd rather do. Sometimes I had to pinch myself to see if this was real. I finally met a good man.

It was getting very late and the last time I heard from Judas was three or four hours ago. I began to worry, and before I knew it, it was 8 am. I decided to call but the phone kept ringing out. I couldn't understand what was going on. My anxiety started to get the best of me. All I could think of was Judas getting into a car accident, in a hospital somewhere and because we weren't married I wouldn't be informed. I really didn't want to ask Tamia because I was ashamed that I didn't know. But I needed closure. I couldn't eat or sleep for the past few weeks.

After 30 days, I finally got the nerve to ask Tamia's boyfriend. You could tell that John didn't want to tell me what he knew but I told him I needed to know. It was only right for him to tell me what was going on. John asked me if I was sitting down, and once I heard those words, I knew it wouldn't be good. I just didn't know how bad it was going to be.

"Well, Brooklyn, Judas went home and got married to his son's mom." My heart just dropped to the floor. I was in disbelief. Everything he told me was a lie. *How could I be such a fool? I was deceived. Why didn't I see this coming?* There were a lot of unanswered questions, but I guess some questions don't need to be answered. I can see that John was so worried about me that he kept on checking on me after he told me what was going on. I was very grateful. I didn't know how I was going to get through this but with John and Tamia's support, it made it easier. He just happened to call Tamia while in my presence. All I could hear was his friend in the background, asking what I looked like and if we could exchange numbers. I wasn't really ready to move on but I was so full of anger, I decided to go ahead and do it.

Tamia said, "Girl he is so cute, he's more your type." Tamia was very upset about the way Judas just ghosted me after expressing how much he loved me. I can't lie, James became a big distraction for me. He took the pain away for a few hours during the day, but it would always find its way back to my heart. He talked about getting into the music industry and how he wanted to become a producer. He was very handsome, but he was what I was used to. The swag, the good looks, and the New York hustle didn't make me feel safe. I didn't want to get my heart broken again. However, he was very respectful and sweet to me. We began to talk for hours, getting to know each other more and more, but my heart was sold by the dream Judas planned for me. How can he do this to me? I was deceived.

It wasn't until September that I received a letter explaining what happened and boy, was I young and naïve. I wanted this relationship more than anything. See, a man doesn't have to lie to a woman. We lie to ourselves. I wanted this so badly that I believed a lie, that he only married his son's mother because she needed his help and she didn't love him. Claiming that it was his responsibility to make sure she was ok. If she wasn't good, then his son wasn't good. I didn't have kids at that time, but I had empathy for him and his situation. My calls to James lessened in numbers. What was I doing? Why was I so hooked on this square-looking guy? James was the total opposite. James had swag and understood me but he was a lady's man, and I was looking to settle down. I wrote Judas back stating he could call me. Why did I do that? All of my feelings came back to the surface once I heard his voice.

I had a heart-to-heart conversation with my mother about the whole situation and she responded by telling me she understood my pain, but at the end of the day, he was now a married man. That alone changed everything. Wow, that was my reality. The man I love; I can't even be with because he's married now. One decision can change your whole life. I just put my head down and cried because the reality was that I could no longer be with him unless he got a divorce. That can take months or years. He eventually called me so that we could have this conversation over the phone and not on paper.

"I'm so happy to hear your voice," Judas said.

"I'm happy to hear yours as well. How could you ghost me and say you love me? Make it make sense to me." I cried.

"I can't do that but I know I love you and want to make us right again," he replied. I wanted to give him that chance, but with him being married, that would be very difficult. We kept in touch here and there because I didn't want to get attached to him until I knew it was right. It was a Saturday morning and I was on the D train when I received a call but I was unable to pick up because the train was under the tunnel. I checked my voicemail. It was a woman named Kim. She proceeded to tell me Judas was her husband and she wanted to know what was going on. I was confused - if she really didn't want this relationship and he married her to help, why call me?

We weren't in a relationship, so I didn't call her back; I waited for him to call me to tell me what was going on. I received another call, only this time it was my sister telling me that a lady named Kim called asking what was going on with Judas and me. She proceeded to say he was a big cheater and that he was in a relationship with two other women. She also said when she threw him out he wouldn't have peanuts. It sounds to me like she meant business and a woman who cares. Judas looks more like a liar.

My sister explained that Judas and I were no longer together because he left me and married her. "Right now, they're just friends." I was so confused. Did he just lie to me about the marriage? Who was this man? Once again, something isn't right. We weren't together, so I just fell back from talking to him and let him handle his business. Once he got the divorce we could revisit this relationship. Eventually, Kim moved back home with her family, and they had to wait a year to get a divorce. In my head, I believed if he were for me, he would come back around. A year passed and we made it official. Let the lies continue.

Deceived wasn't the word. More like manipulation. But I can only go by speculation of another, another that may love him like I. I'm nothing but a victim, caught in his web of lies.

CHAPTER FOUR

Fairy-Tale World

It was about 7 am when I received a phone call. I picked up and Judas was on the other end. "Hello?"

"Hello bae, guess what? I received my divorce papers today in the mail," he told me excitedly.

I asked, "How do you feel?"

"I feel great, now we can start our lives together." I couldn't believe this was happening; I was finally getting what I had been waiting for so long. Should I even feel rejoiceful? But this is the man I thought was for me. So I should be happy but unfortunately, I had mixed emotions.

We decided to see each other as often as we could so that we could rekindle what we had. Also, so that we would never miss each other. Things were going superbly. His behavior was very reassuring. He even made me feel wanted and valued. In my eyes, he could do no wrong. This is what most people call the "butterfly stage" where there are red flags and all of a sudden, you're diagnosed with being color blind. You see pink instead of red. That's the scary part because you don't understand that you're setting yourself up for failure.

We were months in and the relationship was going well. We were both making an effort to see and spend quality time with one another. I began working on Flatbush Ave in this big, beautiful salon. I was gaining more clientele, so there would be times I stayed very late. Sometimes, when Judas came into town to see me, he would pick me up from work. Everyone was a little familiar with who he was to me. On this particular Saturday, I was on my last client, trying to finish up so I could catch that 7-pm 44 bus to go home because Judas couldn't come that weekend. As I started to curl my client's hair, I heard everyone screaming so I looked back to see what was going on (because I'm nosy). I saw Judas on one knee with this beautiful ring in his hand.

"Brooklyn, will you marry me?" My heart was racing, the tears were falling from my eyes. I responded with a loud YES. I kissed him and was in disbelief for the rest of the night. Let's face it, this was a woman's dream - to marry the man she loves - and the way he asked me was out of a fairy-tale book. Everyone around was so happy for me, except Tamia. I wasn't sure why, but I know she didn't like the way he handled the marriage issue. I was too excited to really sit and think about it. I know, I know, I should think about why my friend wasn't really happy for me, but I felt I loved him and she should support me no matter if she agreed. All I was thinking about was being Mrs. Fraud. On a warm Monday morning, I received a call from Tamia expressing how she really felt about my situation. She felt I was a fool to take

Judas back. I can't lie - I really understood why but I was in a defensive mood, and I couldn't receive anything she was saying to me. The result of our conversation was that Tamia and I were no longer friends, and I felt terrible. She was the reason why we were together. I wanted her to be a part of it. I would get in my feelings as I started planning for the wedding. I could see the groomsmen wearing blue and my bridesmaids wearing candy apple green as the beautiful flower girls dropped flowers for me to come down the aisle with my dad. I would fantasize about it daily. *Oh my, this is really happening. I'm about to be off the market.*

Weeks passed by, and I woke up one morning unable to hold anything down. I initially thought it was anxiety stemming from all the wedding plans, but I was totally wrong. I had enough and I decided to go see my doctor. I was blindsided by unforeseen news. We were expecting a baby. Judas came to see me that weekend. As we lay in the bed, I showed him my results. He was so excited. Everything felt so right. I was about to start my own little family. All I could do was thank God for my blessings. Judas was unable to take me to my monthly appointments so my cousin stepped up and took me. About three months into the pregnancy I was told we were having a baby girl. I was so happy to be having a healthy baby. That's all that mattered. Months have gone by and everything seems to be going well. I received a phone call from my brother one afternoon. He was very upset with me and didn't want me to get into his business with his daughter. We got into a big disagreement and it left me feeling very sad. I was only seven months pregnant when I was awakened by contractions. I was very nervous as I lay there, waiting for the doctor to arrive. As the doctor entered the room he said, "Well, young lady, you're experiencing premature labor. We will give you meds to stop the contractions but I'm putting you on bed rest until you have the baby." I tried to take it easy and not stress myself. I put aside my feelings about the issues I had with my brother to make sure I made it to full term.

It was a Tuesday morning when I heard my mother screaming at the top of her lungs because a plane just went into one of the twin towers. We were all confused about what was going on. As we tried to get some information from the news, Judas called to check on us. Seventeen minutes later, another plane crashed into tower two. We were in disbelief. Judas was trying to comfort me, but after seeing the first tower go down I lost it. My anxiety was through the roof by the time the second tower went down. I began to think about the possibility of Judas going to war. What would I do without him? This was a very sad day for Americans, and I was bringing a child into this world. At this point, I was having all kinds of mixed emotions.

One afternoon, Judas called to initiate a serious conversation about us getting married before the baby was born. He felt it would be the right thing to do. I didn't really see the point if we were already booked to have our big wedding the following year but I was all for it. He came a few weeks later and we took the longest forty-five-minute drive to Queens. My sister came along as a witness. I was so nervous and excited. *Is this really happening? I have waited for this day ever since we met.* I felt all that I went through was worth it. Judas had to assist me out of the car. I wobbled my little way into that courthouse. The line was way out the door. I saw we weren't the only couple getting married today. We presented our paperwork and sat down only to be called. As we sat there I could see something was going on with Judas. He wasn't himself. I turned and asked him, "What's wrong?"

He looked at me and said, "I don't think we should get married." My mouth dropped. Did this man just bring me all the way to the courthouse just to say he didn't want to get married? All I could do was cry. I was so full of disappointment. My sister was forty-five hot. I had to hold her back from hurting him. He called out, "Brooklyn, I just don't want to move fast."

I responded, "What does that mean? You proposed already. Did you bring me up here to make me look like a fool? Because you succeeded. Just take me home." We drove home in silence. I had no words for the embarrassment I felt. At this time I just felt Judas was a bag of confusion and you know what they say God is not the author of confusion. So God must not be in this. But you know me, I looked past that. The flag was pink.

The very next morning, I woke up to a kiss on the forehead, and Judas stated he was very nervous about getting married again as if I was being punished for his first marriage.

I replied, "It's okay, I will never pressure a man to marry me."

"Let's go now," he said.

I yelled out, "Hell no! So you can embarrass me like yesterday? No thanks. Don't pity me, I will be okay like I said." He convinced me that he wanted to get married anyway and that he was just scared. We made that long forty-five-minute ride back to Queens so that we could say "We do." My cousin was my witness this time because my sister wasn't having it. All the excitement was stolen from me by the drama the day before, but I had no clue what was waiting for me.

My princess was born a few weeks later, and that was the best day of my life. I had an appointment that day, and the doctor told me he was going to induce my labor so that way he could call the Red Cross and Judas could be there. Unfortunately, I had the baby before Judas arrived. He came to see her for a few hours, but he had to go back until he got permission to take leave. You could see the happiness on his face. He didn't even want to leave. He took so many pictures of her before departing from us.

They say God is not the author of confusion. Confusion was my life, and I was beginning to lose it. Lose the very thing that God blessed me with, which is myself. Who am I? Am I a woman who doesn't know her worth? Is this worth losing me? I guess I was up for the challenge to see. Once again, I didn't pick me.

CHAPTER FIVE

The Wedding Out of A Fairy Tale

Whoever said having a child was easy, wasn't telling the truth. Getting up through the night, feeding, and changing diapers were killing me. Unfortunately, Judas couldn't help me because he was serving in the military and I understood that, but boy, it wasn't easy, so I had to rely on my family. I knew something was going on with me and I was scared to express it. I didn't have a connection to my daughter. My mother gave Sheena her first bath and I can see the joy and excitement in my mother's eyes. Why didn't I feel that? Did I miss something? My mother laid her down to sleep so I could get some rest, but Sheena got up at 1 am, crying her lungs off. I was so done. I was going towards my mom's room to tell her I couldn't do this, but she met me halfway because she heard Sheena crying. My mother came in, asking what was going on and the first thing I said was, "I don't want this baby, take her from me." My mother began to feel bad. She couldn't understand how a mother would say that. I was wondering myself. I couldn't really understand why I was feeling this way but there was a disconnect between Sheena and me.

At my six-week check-up, my doctor began to ask me questions as he examined me. I explained to him that I didn't feel like myself and that I was depressed. "Well, Brooklyn, this sounds like postpartum. I will give you some meds if you think you need it," he said.

"I'm not sure if I need it, but if I feel like I'm not getting better, I will book another appointment." I came home and called Judas to tell him what happened at my appointment. You can tell that he was a little concerned.

"I don't want you taking the bus anymore so I will get you a car," he said. I didn't have my license at the time but you better believe I went to get it. Getting on the bus with a baby and stroller is the hardest thing to do.

As time went on, I started to grow a bond with Sheena. She was loved by so many, and I was grateful for all the help I had. After a while, I decided to go back to work because I couldn't afford to stay at home anymore. Judas couldn't really send me much - about a hundred dollars a month. Let's face it, that wasn't enough to take care of Sheena. I understood he was already paying child support for his son and he wasn't left with much more after that. I made a promise that I would only work three days. Leaving her with her godmother or my sister all day long made me feel really bad. I wished Judas was there to help. As Sheena got a little older, I felt that she needed to be around kids her age, so I decided to put her in daycare part-time. That was all I could afford until my business was able to pick back up. After a while, I had a routine with Sheena. I could run my business and try to be a great mother. I was still going through depression, but planning the big wedding brought me joy. It was only months away and I had to pay for all these things so I had to go into a hustle mode. The only thing Judas had to do was show up with his family. I had to pull some late-night hours. Sometimes I would be there at one or two in the morning. My brother would pull the gate down and lock me in. I wasn't scared to make money.

The wedding was here before you knew it. All the bridesmaids were beautiful. They were a little tired from the bachelorette party. Oh my, that stripper was very entertaining. The DJ yelled out, "Coming before you is Mr. Chocolate!" and dropped the beat. The ladies went wild. All I saw was this handsome, tall glass of water coming towards me. I ran for my life.

My aunt went up to him and said, "You're so lucky I have a skirt on or we would have been on that dance floor." After the entertainment, Mr. Chocolate kissed my hand and said good luck. I didn't know how to take that but it was going down in a few hours, so there was no turning back. My sister who was my matron of honor helped me to get dressed. With her, I didn't have to do anything. She made sure everyone and everything was in place. My Rolls Royce arrived at the venue red carpet style. I felt so beautiful. As I entered the venue, the best man handed me a written note from my husband-to-be. "To my future wife," it said. "Here we are," and that was about how much I could read because the tears began to fall from my eyes. My friends had to read the rest to me. There wasn't a dry eye in the room. It's like I could feel this love from the other room. It was time to walk down that aisle, and I was nervous. Everyone stood on their feet as I came into the room. I could see Judas crying the moment he laid his eyes on me, so I didn't look at him. That was the only way I could make it down that aisle. He gazed deeply into my eyes as he recited his vows and so did I.

The Pastor said, "You may kiss your bride." Everyone was full of excitement. I was finally Mrs. Fraud.

We stepped into the reception while the DJ played "Next, Wifey." Our first dance was to endless love. He looked deep into my eyes as we danced. It was just a beautiful moment. I was looking around to see if any of Judas's family attended, and no one came. Was that a sign? Maybe they didn't approve of this marriage. I just know my family will have many questions at the end of the night. I continued to have a great time. Judas wasn't really a dancer but I was, so I stayed on the dance floor all night. I didn't want the night to end. Unfortunately, we didn't have a honeymoon, but I was hoping in the near future we could. The love we made that night felt so different for me. It was like I belonged to him and he belonged to me, and we were one, hoping no man could come between.

Soon, we found ourselves pregnant again. I guess the love we made was extra special because a baby was produced that night. What was I going to do? Sheena wasn't even one. Even though I hadn't healed from my postpartum fully, I felt I would be ok. I was hoping for a prince.

It was Sheena's first birthday, and she wasn't feeling well. She had a high fever of 101. I gave her Tylenol to take the fever down. She started turning blue. I drove to the hospital within 10 minutes. The Nurse told me I got there right on time because she needed oxygen. They admitted her asap. I called Judas to inform him what was going on. She had to stay for three days, and it felt like the longest three days of my life. Sheena was diagnosed with asthma. On the way home, reality kicked in. I was doing this alone. I understood that Judas was serving our country but it felt lonely. When Sheena came home, I threw her a big birthday party. I was happy because Judas was able to celebrate with us. My beautiful family was together again. At the end of the night, the party turned into an adult party. We partied until 10 pm. She received so many gifts that I had to get a storage unit. Sheena didn't need any toys for a while.

So many blessings from this wedding. When depression tried to take my mind, joy, peace, and happiness filled my heart. So much so that a baby was made; it may be insane to think this was the answer to my emptiness. But I was ready for what was to come, feeling worthless, and unvalued, hoping things would change but unfortunately, things remained the same and worse.

CHAPTER SIX

Let The Lies Begin

It was Thanksgiving and I was about five months pregnant. I was having my prince that I wanted. Judas was coming down to join us for the holiday. I hadn't seen him since Sheena's birthday, so this is well overdue. My mother and I stood up all night trying to cook Thanksgiving dinner. Judas loved my mother's cooking. He couldn't wait to dive into his plate. Everyone came over to join the fun. We played board games and cards. I realized I wasn't good at cards. My nephew began laughing at me for putting down the wrong cards. Judas had to teach me how to play. He was officially part of the family. Judas fell into his daddy position and put Sheena down for bed. It felt reassuring to receive the support I needed from him. Judas only had a few more hours to spend with me. He went into the shower while I fed Sheena. I noticed his phone kept going off and the ringer was on silent. I decided to check the voicemail.

All I heard on the other end of the phone was, "Hey baby, can't wait to see you, I love you." There was another voicemail so I decided to check that one as well.

Another woman said, "I just want to say I love you." Wait, was I hearing things? I played the voicemails three times just to make sure. I wanted to be wrong so badly. My heart dropped to the floor and rage took over.

I went to the bathroom and threw the brushes and combs into the tub where he was taking a shower as I cried, "Get the fuck out of my house! I can't believe you would do this to me!" Judas looked as if he saw a ghost.

He responded by saying, "Baby, what's wrong? What did I do to make you so upset?"

"You know exactly what you did. I want you to take your shit and leave," I told him. You could hear him turning the water off. He got out quietly, packed his things, and left my mom's house. He tried to explain right before leaving. I looked at him and said, "At this point, there is nothing you can say to me." I was full of anger. He kissed the baby goodbye and drove all the way home. I was unable to sleep throughout the night. All I did was cry. I felt as if I didn't even know this man. He'd been living a double life. I spent thirty thousand dollars on a wedding that lasted five minutes. What was I going to do? It was like I lost myself. I was pregnant - who was going to want a young woman with two kids already? I was scared to raise these children alone.

Eventually, I cried myself to sleep. I had no energy the next morning. I got up to use the bathroom. As I was using the restroom, I felt something coming out of me. It looked like a balloon. Then the water came down my leg. I knew what this meant but it was way too early for this to be happening. I rushed to call the doctor to tell him my water had broken. He responded by saying to meet him at the hospital. My oldest brother came to take me to the hospital. He ran every red light there was just to get me there. He even stayed with me for a while. There I was, about to have my second child by myself. How can one be married and feel so alone?

As I waited for the doctor to come I prayed, "Lord, I know I haven't made the best decisions, but please let my baby be ok." I was living in regret. It was so hard for me to deal with. I kept asking the Lord, why me? My father came to see me and I felt like a little girl again. He was going to take care of everything. For a moment, I wanted to be a kid again, but we knew that wasn't happening.

My doctor arrived and said, "I want you to understand that you're only five months pregnant and the baby may not make it."

I screamed out, "NOOOOOOO! Please help my baby!" He said he would do everything he could. I fell into a depression. Everything was going from bad to worse. The contractions began intensifying as the doctor examined me, revealing I was only five cm dilated. About fifteen minutes later, I felt as if I had to push. It was like I went from five to ten that quick. I decided to push whether or not the doctor was there. I gave a hard push and my baby boy was born. I lifted him up and placed him on my chest. I asked my dad to call the doctor or nurse. I could see his little body trying to breathe. The nurse came to take him and clean him up. I waited for a while for them to bring him back, and I didn't understand what was taking so long. My doctor came to me with sad news.

"Mrs. Fraud, there's no easy way to say this but your son didn't make it," the doctor said. I shouted out with a piercing scream. I was hoping all of this was a dream, but the reality was I lost my baby boy. My doctor brought my son so I could say my goodbyes. It was very painful knowing I was so upset last night that it may have led me here. Maybe if I didn't check Judas's phone, I would still have my baby.

"Lord, take this pain from me!" I screamed out. I was able to take pictures and spend time with him. Eventually, the nurse came to take him from me. I wouldn't wish this feeling on anyone. I felt so incomplete, but I knew it was time to let go. I was told by the nurse that I was being placed in another room. I tried to get some sleep. About three hours later, I was given a roommate. I could hear her baby crying and all I could think about was my son.

Why would they put me in a room with someone who has their baby? I tried to ignore the cries but it was impossible. I had a mental break. The doctor gave me something so I could sleep. By the time I woke up, the young lady was removed from my room. I took this time to think about my next move. I was so scared to live alone and ashamed to say my marriage failed already, so I decided to make my marriage work. I couldn't help but feel as if I was grieving by myself. He didn't express any emotions. He couldn't even look at me. The shame was all over his face.

A mother who loses her son loses a part of herself that she can never get back, back to a place where her heart beats triple times, of the excitement of seeing her son grow into a man. You took that from me with your dishonesty, and now I will never see the man that he was supposed to be. I'm letting my loneliness get the best of me. I stayed. I'm a fool but, at this point, I don't know what I should do.

CHAPTER SEVEN

She Didn't Want To Be Second

I was finally back at work, enjoying slaying my clients. trying to take my mind off of things. That brings me immense joy, despite the mix of my depression. Judas wasn't really happy about me still living in New York. He'd been complaining about us living apart. He said he didn't get married for us to live in different states. I knew he would just cheat on me again if we stayed apart and I can't lie I was scared of that. I agreed with him, but the trust in me wasn't there. How could I leave my family, where I feel safe, to be with a man who made me feel unsafe? Choosing to go felt like a death sentence. I know I should be going. Well, that's easier said than done.

A decision had to be made within the next month. I guessed I would be relocating. The reality hit hard when Judas began loading my belongings into the U-haul truck. After a few weeks, I became accustomed to my new life. The downfall was that I was unable to work. We couldn't afford a babysitter so the struggle became real. There were occasions when we had to convert change into dollars just so we could eat, and when we ran out of change, we had to turn to my mother and brother for money. They would send us two to three hundred for groceries. It was a very humbling moment for Judas and me. I was starting to think this wasn't the best decision for our family. But I allowed him to lead the family; after all, who was I to make decisions when I couldn't contribute financially? I tried to support him in any way I could.

Judas came to me and said he would like for his son to come live with us but how can we do that if we're struggling? I told him let's try the summer first. I knew with him working all day I would have to step up to the plate to help my husband. I handed over the cell phone, which my mom had provided for me so that he could reach us on the landline. He would call to check on us during the day to make sure we were okay and to make sure we didn't need anything. I loved that about him. I was bored sitting at home, so I thought some spring cleaning would be great for us. As I was cleaning, I came across a notebook with love letters. This young lady was pouring her heart out. She stated that this was unfair to her and that he was supposed to marry her. She was tired of being second to me. I had no clue that Judas was seeing another woman while dating me. I was wondering if this was the same woman. I wanted to vomit. I couldn't take it anymore. I changed my whole life to be with a liar and a cheater. I called Judas even before reading the rest.

"Hello," he said.

I responded by saying, "You're a cheating, good-for-nothing ass man. You better get home to explain these books of love letters and why you still have them or I will bash that car outside, I promise you." This took me back to the day I lost my son. I was in a full rage. This couldn't be happening to me again. I heard the door opening within five minutes of hanging up.

Judas came in saying, "Let me explain."

"I want the full truth, is this the same woman that we lost the baby over?"

He responded, "Yes, but I told her it was over and that I wanted my marriage." Was I supposed to be happy because you picked me over her? I had all types of emotions running through my body. I just moved here; I left my salon for this shit. Do I pick up and just leave? I called my mother to tell her what just happened and get her advice. She thought it was best to make it work if he had promised to change. The big question was, would he? I found myself replaying the loss of my son over and over after reading these letters. I couldn't keep going through this. My confidence and self-esteem went low. The woman I once was no longer exists. I started looking at every little flaw I had. I felt as if he wanted a skinner light-complexioned woman. I started taking long walks with my daughter around the neighborhood so I can lose some weight. I even started taking these weight loss pills that had my heart racing. I became desperate. His actions started to affect me mentally. Almost losing me scared him a little. He started to show me that he wanted to work on his marriage. The relationship got a little better but financially we were not. I overheard him talking to his friend on the phone about someone coming to repossess the car. I knew we were doing bad but I didn't think it was that bad. I felt I needed to do something so I decided to ask my mom. I know his pride kicked in, but we desperately needed help. I stood by my husband even though he couldn't take care of us. I would help him in any way I could.

"Hey Mommy, we need your help again," I told my mom. I was very embarrassed to call her with another issue but this wasn't the time to be prideful. We were going to lose the car, which left Sheena and me without a car. My dad called us back and said they would take over the car payments until Judas could catch up on bills. Judas was very humble and grateful for the help. I wasn't used to living like this, and after what I had been going through, I didn't think I could take anymore but boy, was I wrong. I found myself begging to even be touched by Judas. I didn't really understand what was going on. All I could think of was that my husband didn't find me attractive anymore. That the woman that he'd been sleeping with was what he wanted. Should I even keep trying?

One afternoon, Shenna and I went to get some things for the house, and I took the cell phone just in case I needed to call Judas for anything. As I sat in the car, something told me to check the call log because of his strange behavior. I saw a pattern of calls being made by Judas every morning at 5 am. It looked like the calls I used to get. A "Good morning beautiful, enjoy your day," type of call. Sometimes when you know someone really well, you can guess their next move.

I called the number back and there was a woman on the other end. I went on to ask her who she was and if she was sleeping with my husband. She told me her name was Sparkle and that I needed to ask him.

"No, I am asking you. As a matter of fact, where do you live or work so I can come see you? Did you know he was married?" I asked.

She replied, "Once again, I told you, you need to ask him." Well, that told me a lot. I went straight to Judas. It became really physical. I slapped him and the next thing you know, we're choking and hitting each other. Did I get married for this? I found myself in this unwanted place. I started to cry and asked him if he wanted to be with her, and if he did, I would be willing to walk away from this right now? I told him if he didn't want to be with her, he should call her and tell her it was over. He proceeded to call Sparkle to prove he didn't want what they had and make it clear he wasn't leaving me. I could hear the phone ringing.

She picked up with excitement in her voice. "Hello?"

Judas was straightforward and said, "I can no longer see you and be in contact with you. I love my wife and I don't want to hurt her."

She said, "Okay, and I understand." Our home would never be the same. What we had became very toxic.

I woke up the next morning feeling like I messed up my life marrying this man. My mindset was it was too late to leave. I no longer had a job, nor did I have any money. I couldn't even feed my child. I was losing it. I felt that I needed to get out of the house to think of my next plan. I went window shopping with Sheena. I stayed in the mall for about two hours. I pulled up and I saw Judas's car outside the house. He came home early. Maybe he wanted to talk. When I entered the house I could tell that he was talking to someone. I came in right in time to hear my husband telling Sparkle that I made him say that and that he didn't mean it. My heart dropped to the floor. I'm surprised I didn't have a heart attack. I went into a rage again. I became physical with him. It felt like I completely lost control. I was consumed with the urge to harm him, but I had Sheena and I wasn't going to jail behind a liar. Why would he marry me? This woman isn't even the one we lost our child because of. She's entirely a different woman. Judas was living a double life. I lost my friend Tamia because I married him. I was mentally drained. I didn't have a fight in me anymore. I gave up mentally but I was hoping that he would see my worth and learn to love me. I became more insecure. I didn't trust anything he said so our relationship became more toxic and neither of us was ready to give up.

Sometimes you really don't know a person until you become one. One sound, one beat, to discover the deceit. The deceit of lies of every word that comes out of their mouth. The amount of souls that they're connected to and now intertwined with yours. Now toxic, too many demons fighting yours. It's a legion. It's screaming exorcism. Know who you're dealing with before you lay;

you might be a fool and just stay. I did.

CHAPTER EIGHT

Toxic Behavior Produces Toxicity

We now found ourselves in a very toxic relationship. When it was good, it was good, but when it was bad, it was bad. I opened my own daycare within our home and I would work some days in a salon for extra cash. Judas would deploy for six months, so it gave us a break from our fighting. With me working again, my self-esteem started to build back up. The most painful feeling is when someone makes you feel you're a burden. Judas was great at making me feel this way. His favorite statement was I should have a Lexus by now as if he didn't have us, he could afford it. His mindset was very money-driven while I valued family. One day when I came into work there was this handsome man looking at me so I looked away. I didn't want to have any eye contact. I knew that would open doors I didn't want to open, so I went about my business, working on my clients. The next day I received flowers. It said it was from a secret admirer. I knew exactly who it was from. I was smiling on the inside because it had been a long time since Judas made me feel special. He came over to ask me if I received the flowers. I responded with yes and a big smile on my face. I also thanked him and told him I was married and couldn't take them. He said he understood, but the next day I received lunch. I don't think he really cared. That was a "me" problem, not his.

After that day, I knew I had to stay away. This would be a big problem for me and my marriage. I can't lie, it stroked my ego. When Judas came home, I had a new attitude. I forgot who I was because of all the cheating and lies I accepted. I second-guessed myself. I didn't know my worth, and when another man could see something my husband couldn't, it made me feel great. He noticed a change in me and I was honest with him about the man sending me flowers and lunch. You could see he couldn't really handle it. I told him I wasn't putting up with the mistreatment anymore. Judas went as far as to talk to my auntie. He told her that he was willing to change, and for a while, I saw it. It didn't last long, but as usual, I lied to myself.

Judas had to deploy for a while again. He would go back and forth out to sea, so I was a single parent most of the time. While he was away, he called me to check on us and to vent about not knowing where his son was. "Hey babe, can you do me a favor? Can you call my ex-wife to check on my son?" he asked.

I responded, "I'm uncomfortable calling because you didn't have a sit down with me and your ex-wife to make sure she was ok with me calling." I could tell he wasn't happy with my responses, but it was my truth. I thought he would understand. Until I received a call from a family member expressing to me that a woman was calling, looking for my son Sean.

"What was her name?" I asked. I realized right there I wasn't ready to hear the answer. It was said to be Sherae. Why am I reliving the death of my son again? "Sherae was the woman that Judas was cheating on me with when we lost the baby," I said. This man was still messing with her. I was convinced that he hated me. No way could I believe he loved me. Judas was on deployment so I had to wait until he called me, which was a few hours and felt like years. I was walking back and forth thinking about what I was going to say. I wasn't able to give Sheena the best of me because I was so broken. It was about 6 pm when I heard the phone ring.

"Hello babe" was the first thing he said to me.

I yelled out loud, "Don't 'hello babe' me! Why did you have that woman Sharae call looking for our son? You mean to tell me you couldn't have your mother do it? You're still in contact with this woman even though we lost our son due to your actions? You have to be kidding me! I'm fucking done. Done with you and your shit. I have stayed through all your bullshit and for what? Clearly, you don't care about me or this marriage."

"No babe, I was desperate to find out what was going on with my son, and you didn't want to do it. I needed help but there is nothing going on with us I promise. I will not call her again. Please stop," he stated. Once again, I knew he was lying, but I didn't leave. Besides, where would I go? I didn't have any money.

My mother said, "At least he's not like your father," like that made it any better. I had to become numb in order to deal with this whole relationship. I loved Judas so much that I couldn't see life without him, even if it was dysfunctional.

Judas was due to come back from deployment but Hurricane Katrina hit so hard in Louisiana that the ship had to go help rescue families. He came home about two weeks later. Sheena and I went to the ship port to pick him up. You could tell he was happy to see us. We made love that whole night. It's been a long time since he has even touched me like that. That weekend, we went to retrieve his son so he could live with us. I noticed he kept his phone in between his legs as if he didn't want me to see who was calling. I was trying not to ruin the moment so I kept it to myself. We stayed about four days so that Judas could spend time with family. It was a long, quiet ride back home. When we arrived home, I showed Sean his room. I could see this was a lot for him. I didn't want to overwhelm him so I left him to get adjusted. Judas expressed that he was so happy that Sean was with us and that his family was complete. Call me bitter, but why was he so happy because we were all together and complete? Our son was gone and we would never get him back, so we'd never be fully complete. I knew in my heart that he wasn't grieving like I was because of that statement.

Weeks went by and I noticed my menstrual cycle hadn't come. I decided to take a pregnancy test to confirm my thoughts. A few minutes later, I saw two blue lines. We were pregnant. I didn't know if I should be thrilled or scared. The truth was, my husband showed me over and over that this marriage meant nothing to him. At this point, I didn't care what he felt. I was having my baby, even if I had to do it by myself. I built the nerves to tell him, and to my surprise, he was very happy to hear that our family was expanding. At my three-month mark, I was told I was having another boy. I may have lost my first son but I received a blessing with another one.

When I told Judas the sex of the baby, you could see that he was disappointed because he said, "You need to check that again." I just laughed and walked away. One evening, Judas called to inform me we were getting stationed in New Jersey. That was all heard. I was ready to go back up north to be near my family. I knew going up that way I would have a lot of help.

Once again, I had to start over with building my business. Because I had experience in early childcare, I applied to the school on base. Not having money or a job left Judas with a little bit of control. This has become a very humble moment for me. He was out there with different women and I couldn't get rooted anywhere because of all this moving. Some days I felt helpless but I kept God's word in my heart. I still had hope that my marriage would turn around for the better. It was a beautiful day to move. The sun was shining as if that was a good sign that this move was going to be good for us. I received a call that I got a job at the CDC. It was great for Sheena and me to go to work together and Sean went to the after-school program. Things were looking bright here. We took trips to see my family at least once or twice a month. Judas and I were respectful to one another at this time. Could it be he's finally trying and being faithful? You will never know with him. Things can be going well and five minutes later he will change up on you.

It was a Thursday morning when I went to work and started having contractions. I was terrified because I was only eight months pregnant. After losing a child the same way, you can't help but panic. Judas came to my job to take me to the hospital. When the doctor entered the room, he explained that I was going into labor but my baby seemed to be doing well. I needed to hear that good news. That gave me the confidence I needed to be strong. This was the first child that Judas was able to experience with me.

Johnson was born at four pounds five ounces at 8 pm that night. He looked just like his brother. Back at home, my sister and mother were organizing a baby shower for me. I was surrounded by gifts and love. Monday morning, I checked my baby's temperature and it was very low, scaring me. Johnson had to be admitted to the hospital and stayed there for two weeks. Every day I got up to breastfeed Johnson while Judas went to work. Some days I took Sheena and Sean to visit their younger brother Johnson. Six months later, Judas was asked to go to Iraq which would leave me with all three kids to raise alone. It was a big decision to make. Many were still losing their lives but Judas decided not to go, causing us to have to pick a new duty station in North Carolina the following year. Before leaving New Jersey, we threw Johnson his first birthday party. We turnt up and celebrated. Before the night ended, Sheena and her friend decided to call the police and the whole base's police department showed up and had to check the house. I was so upset at first but had to laugh. After they left, the party resumed again.

Something beautiful was produced out of toxic love. Hoping and praying it would not become toxic. See, a house divided will not stand, and let's face it, we were divided. He was living his truth and I was living his lie. It was just a matter of time til I said goodbye.

CHAPTER NINE

Seeking Help From The Church

After dropping Sean off with his mother for the summer and driving eight hours, we finally saw the sign reading "Welcome to North Carolina." Driving with two kids and one adult child is the hardest thing to do. I was burnt out with all the crying from Johnson and Sheena laughing at Judas making jokes. All I wanted to do was get some rest, but that was impossible without our household goods and beds. Judas went to the office to get our keys to our new place. Once we received the keys, we went straight to the house. Sheena stepped out of the car into an ant hole. I had no idea what had happened until I saw all these ants running all over her feet. I dusted them off and took her into the house but that didn't stop her from picking her new room. The smile on her face was priceless. That night we all slept in one room on an air mattress. Bright and early around 8 am, our household goods were delivered, and Judas had to check in at his new duty station. He came home around lunch to break the bad news. He was leaving for deployment the next day. I was deeply upset. How was I going to take care of a toddler and a five-year-old? I also had to set up our brand-new house, but you know what they say, when duty calls, you gotta go. Judas left for six months, leaving me to learn to survive once more on my own. I enrolled Sheena in school and Johnson in daycare, and soon after, I found a job and a church to go to.

Church kept me grounded and in prayer. I started confiding in my pastor about the issues I faced in my marriage. I was able to build my life in North Carolina and make it my home, but Sheena was having a hard time adjusting. She would come home crying from the bullying she started to experience at school. As time passed, she developed friends within the church. We even encountered people who were stationed with us in New Jersey, making the feeling of being in North Carolina better. I would call from time to time to check on Sean and one afternoon his mom said to me he would not return to us. She enrolled him in school already. I knew Judas was going to be upset with this news but I'm a mom, I understood. Besides, Judas was still paying child support while he was living with us, so we were paying double which left us financially struggling.

There were times Judas would often make me feel bad for his mistakes and decisions. When Judas finally came back, I had to adjust to his presence at home. He even started going to church with me. The pastor pulled us aside and suggested marriage counseling for us. The first meeting got straight to the point of things.

"Who taught you how to love?" he asked. We both said our parents, leading to the second question. "Are your parents still married?" I said yes, my parents were technically married but only on paper. Judas on the other hand said no. "So you don't know what love looks like…" Pastor said, opening up my eyes that we were never properly taught how to love.

We tried to continue marriage counseling, but with Judas's busy schedule it was hard to commit to a specific day, and maybe it wasn't as important to him as it was for me. His life never changed. He had a job and a life everywhere we went; I didn't. I only had him and the kids. This left our marriage once again vulnerable. I noticed Judas started making friends, but one of them stood out the most, Delilah. I kept an eye on his behavior and tried not to let it rattle me, but a person can only take so much.

Around November that year, Judas asked me to go to the Navy ball. I was excited since we hadn't gone out on dates or had time for ourselves. I felt good that night, I was wearing a black cocktail dress and red pumps. You couldn't tell me anything. I know I was cute. As we entered the ball, I locked eyes with someone who looked very familiar. I couldn't figure out where I knew her from. I turned my head towards Judas and noticed he had become tense. Now he had my attention. We walked around until we found our table to sit at. We didn't even sit for 5 minutes when Judas got up.

"Hey babe, I'll be right back," Judas said immediately. I saw him walk away and speak to the woman who looked familiar.

"Hey Sharae, can we talk?" he said.

"What now?" she said, annoyed.

"My wife is here and—" Sharae cut him off.

"What does that have to do with me?"

Judas sighed and begged, "Please can we just be civil, I don't want any issues. My wife lost a baby because of our affair, and I think it would be better for the both of us if we didn't speak." Judas came back to the table during the speech of one of the commanders. Twenty minutes passed and music began to play. I wanted to have fun and dance with Judas, but he shot me down and said, "I don't know how to dance, but you go ahead and dance for the both of us." I was a little sad but ended up dancing alone that night. At about 10 pm the babysitter called. Sheena wasn't feeling well, so we left and picked her up along with Johnson. As we rode home, I was in my feelings. It felt like Judas was avoiding me the entire night. It was supposed to be a fun night for us. I questioned myself as we went to bed without words of affirmation. I felt that I lost my husband's affection. Was he even attracted to me? Did I even have his heart?

The next morning there was a thick tension in the air. "Do you think we'll be together when the kids turn 18?" I blurted out.

"Yeah, why not?" he said easily, like we had no problems. As the days progressed, I found no peace within my marriage. I found myself arguing more often with Judas. We fought before church, Bible study, and in front of people, and the only way I could escape was when Judas was deployed. I confided more in church and was able to build a better relationship with God through the influence of the deacons at the church who were married for 20+ years. You could even say that I looked up to them and their marriage. Sheryl and Mike were amazing to the kids and me. Sheryl helped me in any way she could and became my close friend.

One Saturday morning, Judas and I got ready for a pinning ceremony. As we arrived, I saw the same, familiar-looking woman there once again. I didn't say anything, but when Judas and her interacted, I paid attention to their conversation and body language. I didn't think they were friends, nor did I have proof he had some sort of relationship with her.

Judas became unrecognizable to me. He would hang out with people who were disrespectful to their wives and me. His friend Carlos would often sleep around with his colleagues at work. One particular day Judas and I went to visit Carlos and his wife. Things began to go to the left very quickly. After a while, he told his wife to escort me out. I can see the fear in her eyes like she didn't want to, but if she didn't there would have been consequences. He felt a woman should know her place.

"Terrie, you don't have to put me out, I'm leaving".

Judas just sat there in silence, leaving me to defend myself. As we left, Judas criticized me, making excuses for his friend instead, the whole way home. The respect I had for my husband was diminishing. As toxic as Carlos was, he wouldn't allow anyone to talk to his wife that way. It changed the way I viewed Judas as a man. I continued to work and build clientele so that one day I would be able to leave Judas. Things were looking up for me. I even had the opportunity to host a hair and fashion show. Two years later, everything I built would become meaningless. We had to move once more. I was leaving behind my church and my business. Starting life all over again.

Our lies and deceit will always catch up with us in the darkest places. A light will shine and the truth will unveil. The truth was he was never my husband, he was a counterfeit, a fraud that put on a facade. It's like my heart sees it but it takes time for my brain to get it. There I said it. Trust not your heart but the wisdom from God.

CHAPTER TEN

Welcome Back To The Commonwealth of Virginia

I never thought I'd see this place again. All I could remember was hurt and pain. Hopefully, this time around things will be better. Our destination—Portsmouth, Virginia. Judas had two weeks off before reporting back to work, so we spent it getting the house together. We set up a space within my home to service clients. It took some time and we adjusted well, but because I didn't know anyone, I realized I needed to find a salon to work in. It's always easy for Judas to bounce back. He gets paid no matter where he goes. For me, it's hard physically and mentally. Eventually, I found a salon, and my only downfall—commission… I was my own boss and having to answer to someone wasn't something I was used to anymore, but I made the best of it. Through this journey, I made friends and met great stylists. After six months I met a nail tech, Nicole. She was setting up her own shop and she asked me to come along with her. Even though we didn't know each other very long, I gave it a shot and it was the best decision I ever made.

As time progressed, I was able to build a clientele through Nicole's clients. Things between Judas and I weren't great. I just tried my best to ignore the phone calls he was receiving from other women. I convinced myself that what I didn't know wouldn't hurt me. After all, where could I go? I had been saying I would leave for years, and it no longer holds any weight. He didn't even pay me any attention. My relationship became more of a chore to me. What we had wasn't marriage.

I joined a group of women in the neighborhood, becoming close to one of the wives in particular named Carrie. We had a lot in common, we both had children in the same grade as well. Carrie introduced me to a new church. It was nice but eventually, I sought out something different. While looking for another church, Nicole recommended one to me. This was a small intimate church and immediately, it felt like home. I had a goal set in place to not depend on Judas for anything. As time went on, I became the co-owner of The Beauty Bar, and it felt like I had a purpose working with Nicole. I was serving at church whether Judas came or not, it gave me peace for a while.

Carrie and I became so close that I started venting to her about what was really going on in my marriage. I can tell that she can only relate as far as being a military spouse but as for the infidelity, her husband was faithful. She made me feel comfortable without judgment. I can tell that Judas was up to his old tricks again. His movement changes, every time he has a side chic. When my nephew came to live with me, I became distracted from paying attention to Judas cheating. So, it was easy for Judas to do his thing. This is where the mental and physical abuse of myself began. I didn't tell anyone because I didn't want anyone to think I was crazy. The truth is, I was going mad. I kept my cool because I had no proof, oh you better believe I eventually started to watch.

One evening, Judas took the kids to the park, but he left his phone on the charger. His phone kept vibrating and each time I turned my head I saw the notification. The name Nikki would appear at the top. When he came back home, it took everything within me not to ask who Nikki was. Besides, it's not like my stupid self was gonna leave anyways… As we lay down to rest, Judas was clearly in distress; he didn't know if I had gone through his phone or not. Four days later, I was rattled mentally, I needed to know what was going on.

I called Carrie, desperate for answers. We spent what felt like hours getting the phone records and got nowhere. I decided to get answers from his phone. By the time I figured out his password, Judas stormed towards me and grabbed me with force, his face contorted in rage. I felt a pain jolt through my wrist and I winced and begged Judas to stop. Carrie, trying to be the voice of reason, begged us as well to stop. When he wouldn't budge to let me go, I balled my hand into a fist and hit him. As retaliation for my actions, he bent my finger back more and then took the phone. I stood there embarrassed that Carrie witnessed the interaction. I spent the rest of the night in disbelief and couldn't sleep. Judas, trying to justify his actions, said Nikki was just a work colleague, and that I would just be embarrassing him, but I knew it was a lie. Why would he harm me over a work colleague?

On Sunday, I went to church. The first lady asked me what I needed prayer for, I grasped her hand tightly and said, "My marriage." She saw my desperation. After service, she asked me to stay back to talk. I confided in her. I told her I was broke and had nowhere to go.

Her reply was, "God honors marriage. Do you think counseling would work?" But I told her I'd already tried that and it ended in failure. Judas was a cheater and will always be a cheater and I'll always be a dummy if I stay. For the next few months, every time Judas's phone rang I would start to harm and degrade myself. I felt worthless, and suicide was knocking at my door. As I was trying to keep myself together, Sean called and wanted to come and stay with us again. I didn't want Sean to come and see what was going on because he wasn't a baby anymore. I had no say in this decision, so when Sean came, we made space for him in Johnson's room. After some time, it was clear Sean was uncomfortable since we didn't have a proper place for him to sleep. Judas came to me and said it was time to buy a house. I was clearly against this decision. Our home was dysfunctional. To buy a house now was crazy to me. It wasn't made for us as a family, but rather a decision for Sean.

In November of that year, we moved into a five-bedroom

house. Even though I was against it at first, I fell in love with that house. From the cherry wood flooring to the freshly built canvas, I could create out of it. Sean, of course, was able to finally get his privacy. Sheena and Johnson were also clearly excited. The first week I spent time painting the house and gardening. It helped clear my mind from all I was going through. Judas was clearly on his best behavior, and Johnson and Sheena were enjoying school. Things were good for a while… Not the best but not the worst. Until Judas got stationed on a ship and any form of contact with him ceased. I confronted him about it. What if there was an emergency? Judas brushed me off though and said the ship had poor cell service.

Judas brought me and the kids to visit his ship, and while we were there, I was introduced to Khrista and Troy. Due to Judas's reputation, I questioned whether Khrista and my husband had any secret relationship, but as time progressed, it was clear he wasn't her type. Life felt harder with Judas on the ship. I didn't have much help with the kids and it was hard for him to meet their needs, but then again, I should have been used to this by now. I kept myself busy at church, trying to distract myself as much as possible. I didn't get much satisfaction from that, so instead, I sought out more help.

I called military source one, receiving therapy for myself. On the first visit, she asked me what brings me here. I asked her, "Where should I start? I'm unhappy with life, my husband cheats on me every few years or more, and I hit myself when I'm in a rage. I even talk down to myself and I want out of my marriage but I'm a coward." After five sessions, the therapist wanted to meet Judas. Of course, he tried to shoot down the idea, but when he realized that our marriage was on the line, he went. During our session, I cried and tried to express how I felt about his infidelity and how I was treated.

Judas patted my back and said, "Brooklyn, stop crying." The therapist didn't like his response and told Judas he was being condescending. Immediately, he shut down for the rest of the session until it was over and stormed out with no intent of returning. The next morning, he said he would go back to therapy, but it had to be with a different person. That's to show you he couldn't take criticism. So, I sought out a new therapist, specifically a male one for Judas's comfort. When I found one, it was pointless… We attended only two sessions and our marriage was once again in jeopardy. Who cares but me?

See, I was losing it, going insane, abusing myself cause I couldn't handle the rain. When it rains, it pours. not realizing God paid for it all, for all my sins, and sin it was to put a man above him who supplies all my needs.

CHAPTER ELEVEN

Discovering My Worth

"**H**ey babe!" Judas's voice was filled with excitement. "We're going to Cuba!" I was not elated.

"I'm not going to Cuba," I said sternly. I was tired of picking up everything and starting over. Judas was taken back by my response. We compromised and decided that he would go to Cuba for a year instead of having all of us live there for three years. Before leaving, Judas bought me a car, and when we went to church that Sunday, he stood in front of the church, crying and praying that we would be well taken care of. That following Saturday, Judas departed for Cuba.

During his time away, I did some self-reflection. It was clear I had become weak and I needed a way out of this marriage. I carefully constructed how I would leave, saving up money and enrolling in college. I took the time to focus on myself. I joined the PTA to spend more time with my kids and, during this process, I met a man named Thomas during an event.

"Can I have some ketchup, ma'am?" he said to me. I was confused.

"For what, you don't have any food in your hand?" I suppose he was trying to flirt with me. Now he caught my eye. Was it because I felt so neglected in my marriage or has it been a long time since I felt wanted? I walked away from Thomas smiling. Before the night was out, I was invited to a Que event. I got the invite from Thomas.

Judas would call and couldn't reach me. I was growing tired and there was a clear rift in our relationship. When I finally spoke to Judas, I broke things off. He was in disbelief, you could hear it in his voice. Truthfully, things were over a long time ago, but I never said it. When I finally said it, things were clear and I continued to make plans for leaving. The Que's event came around, and I attended it. There I saw Thomas once more. He escorted my friends and me to a table. We were having a blast. I hadn't been out in so long that I forgot what it felt like to just relax and vibe to great music. I had a few good-looking men come up to me for a dance and I nicely declined. Some of the Ques began to dance. I enjoyed watching it. That is one thing that I missed—going to college. I ran off and got married to the wrong man and didn't really experience life. At that time, I thought it wasn't worth it.

The DJ called out the last song of the night. I looked to my right and there he was, Thomas, with hands out, asking me to dance. At first, I refused but he came back dancing in front of me. I said to myself, why not? It was my jam by

Rhianna, "Work." I enjoyed dancing and feeling young again. After the dance, Thomas walked my girlfriends and me to our cars and we parted ways. When I got home, I thought about how much fun I had and how nice it felt for a man to treat me like I mattered. This made me realize I was making the right decision. I deserved love and happiness one day. I needed this boost to keep going forward without looking back. I knew it was time, so I stayed focused on building myself and my business to be independent.

Judas continued to call to check on us even though I told him I was done but the tension was on another level. We would fight every day. It came to the point that I didn't even want to talk to him. I was no longer blindfolded. One morning, Judas called to tell me he was sorry for the way he treated me but it was too late. I heard this before so his words didn't carry any weight. I explained to him that I was tired, tired of being second to the women, the job, our kids, and more. I know he didn't believe me and how could he? I said it so many times hoping he would change his ways, and now I became a joke to him. He even got into the habit of saying, "If you're going to leave, leave. You're only going to get a thousand from me. Good luck." My heart would be crushed, but not this time. I was going to stand on faith. I knew what it felt like to stay but had no idea of what it felt like to leave. I knew it was time for me to love myself.

It was another PTA event, and I ran into Thomas. Our eyes locked and we both smiled. I could tell he was interested but he never said anything. By the end of the event, we got a chance to talk and we exchanged numbers. We began to talk every day about life and what we were going through. We found that safe place within each other to vent. It was so easy to talk to him about anything without being judged about staying so long in this toxic marriage. At that time, I needed that. It helped me value myself and have the courage to keep going. Judas noticed the change in me and he could no longer manipulate me.

My phone rang. It was Judas on the other end. "I've been checking the phone records," he said.

I replied, "Good, keep checking." I don't think he understood how done I was. Was he expecting me to lie? Nope, I'm not him. The truth would set him free. He was full of anger. He called me everything but a child of God. I saw he couldn't handle the type of time he was giving me for years. That summer, I sent the kids to New York so that I could work harder to save money to leave. Judas accused me of sending the kids away to have fun with Thomas. I also told him he couldn't come home. If only he knew I was saving to leave his butt. It was almost six to seven months of back-and-forth fighting. It got worse with his disrespect. I didn't really know him while we were married, and I didn't know him now. When he got back from deployment, I could see his pain. He even spoke about suicide. Even though he hurt me time after time, how could I turn my back on him? I know one would call me a fool, but my heart wouldn't let me do it, and besides, I loved him.

If loving me is wrong, I don't want to be right. I owed that to myself, self-love, that is. What I have is love that hurts, hurts every part of my being, seeing myself dying to be loved, should never be. Being treated like a queen is a must, so with that being said, in God I trust. I'm leaving; I'm worthy. I'm tired of your lust.

CHAPTER TWELVE

Saving The Marriage One Last Time

When Judas came back from Cuba, we started marriage counseling with my church. Our first sessions with Ms. Betty went okay, but we hit just the surface. I wanted answers. I didn't know if I could handle it, but I couldn't go on with all the lies.

Ms. Betty said, "At the next session, we'll put everything on the table no matter how hard it is." I waited so long for this day to happen that I don't know if I can handle the truth. As we sat down in front of Ms. Betty, she asked me what it was that I wanted to know. I turned to Judas and asked if he had an affair with the lady, Nikki, who he told me was just his co-worker. He said yes, and I was not surprised. I replayed that day that he bent my finger back to get the phone. All I could think about was that Judas was willing to hurt me to keep a secret. How can a man who loves his wife do that?

I couldn't go on. It hurt too much. I could see that Judas regretted telling me the truth. The very next day Judas took me to Kay Jewelers to pick out a new ring. I saw one I loved.

I was shocked that he purchased the ring. I felt as if he was trying to buy my love but it felt good so I took the ring, knowing in my heart I wasn't sure about this. I told Judas that I was going to stay away from Thomas, but hearing that made me regret every word. I tried to stick this out, but boy was this hard. I found myself missing my late-night conversations with Thomas, so I decided to call him. Within hours of calling Thomas, Judas found out. He was checking the phone records and became furious. How can he be so upset? Judas used Thomas to play the victim, and all that did was push me further away. I began to harbor resentment about getting back together. This was going to the left, so we needed help ASAP.

Going to another counselor was our decision. She was a Christian-based marriage counselor which was a win for me. In the first sessions, she let us vent and express our feelings. After a while, she came in with questions. One question particularly caught my attention. She proceeded to say, "Why did you withhold sex from your spouse?" I wanted to know this answer for years. Was he not attracted to me anymore? Did I gain weight? I was confused.

Judas replied, "I wanted to punish her." My mouth dropped to the floor. I couldn't believe what I was hearing. Did this man just sit here and say he wanted to punish me as if I were a child? For years I felt like crap and beat myself down, and that was his answer. That was the most wicked, self-centered thing to say. I had to ask myself what I was up against? At this point, I felt he had an ugly heart. Who would see his wife crying for affection and just turn their back to punish her? My truth was the more that was exposed, the more I disliked him. God had been showing me the truth for years. I was lying to myself.

We continued to work on it, but Judas didn't waste any time using Thomas against me as if he was faithful throughout the marriage. I was once again being a fool. He didn't love me; this was just another way to keep me in bondage. I went along with it, hoping things would get better. We would take two steps forward and one back. So, it gave me a little hope.

Judas was now stationed on the other side of Virginia. I was willing to go to have a fresh start. We just wanted the kids to get out of school. He decided to sell the house because he felt Thomas came there. He was behaving childishly, but it was just part of his plan, and I went with the flow. My birthday was coming up and he threw me a surprise birthday party and invited my family and friends. I felt a little special because he had never thrown a party for me. I enjoyed myself but, once again, he didn't come up on the dance floor to dance with me. It's like being in a room full of people and still feeling alone. That's what marriage had been like for all those years. I guess I had a little hope. You can't make someone love you. If the gloves don't fit, you must acquit them. Like they said on the OJ Simpson trial. These gloves didn't fit.

This was getting real, we finally got an offer for the house and we agreed to it. As we were packing our belongings out of the house, I couldn't help but feel as if he didn't want me to come with him. He kept saying he was looking for a place for us to stay but he didn't have any luck. "I think it's best that you go to Georgia to start your life there because I'm going to retire after this," he said. My heart was a little crushed, feeling rejected. Oh, it was just a matter of time until I found out why Judas didn't want me to come there. He turned to me and said, "I have to tell you something. Sharea is my boss, I work for her." I knew I wasn't crazy.

"So that is the reason why you don't want us to come," I replied.

He said, "No, I want you to get your career together. You're always saying you're tired of moving." *Did he just gaslight me?* I said to myself. I had so many questions, like why didn't he tell me this before putting the house on the market? Did he try to get rid of me so that they could spend time together? At this point, I was as hot as fish grease. I shut down all the way and the little hope I had was gone. I was so down that I called myself every bad name. I couldn't help but feel I deserved this. I should've left, and now I really couldn't afford to live on my own. Once again, I had to go with the flow. My self-esteem went left. Here I am again. When will I ever learn? We took a ride out and we got into a big disagreement. Judas tried to bring up Thomas to justify the lies he told me. One thing led to another and we were physically fighting in the car. He began to bleed from his lip and people were looking at us. I was a little scared that I was going to be the one going to jail because he was bleeding.

I cried out, "I'm done! I can't keep going through this."

I moved to Georgia and stayed with my cousin Tammy until we found something of our own. Judas kept leading us on. I kept going to look at every house he would send for us to look at. Judas was playing games with me until he finally told me he would not buy another house. So you can leave me and the house would be yours? I couldn't believe he strung me along, looking for a house he never wanted in the first place. I finally understood what he was doing. He was setting up for a divorce.

By now I was getting prepared for what was to come. I wasted so much time looking for a house that school was about to start and the kids needed a place to stay in order to get them in school. I went out and found an apartment with my cousin Tammy. I got the kids registered for school and found a salon suite to start my business. I was no longer on Judas's time because he was the breadwinner. He would come down and visit the kids but that was about it. We were co-parenting at this point. He would tell me he wanted to get back together but show me the opposite. I was growing stranger and stranger. There were days I second-guessed myself but God kept encouraging me. One day, Judas came to visit around his birthday and to bring our things out of storage. He only came with half of our things, stating that this was the biggest truck they had. My son and I only had our mattress while Tammy gave my daughter a bed to sleep on. I was so upset but I didn't have the money or someone to help me get those things out. A humbling moment for me.

I found myself questioning God and the reason for him showing me everything Judas was doing to me because I was suffering.

The very next day I tried to hang myself. Judas came into the bathroom in time to stop me. I was at my lowest. He left the day before his birthday. I told the kids to call him on his birthday but there was no answer all day. I found out he was in Vegas with another woman. Judas never took me on a vacation. I guess it's true when they say a man would do what you allow them to do. We hadn't even discussed divorce yet, but here he was, on a vacation with another woman. What doesn't kill you will make you stronger.

After all this, I knew I needed to find a church. I got invited to a church by a client of mine. When I got there, I realized she was the first lady of the church. I laughed because the whole time I was doing her hair not once did she say she was the pastor's wife. God would give you what you need and he saved me from myself. I had a salon that I couldn't really afford, so I worked at Smart Styles until I built a clientele. Every time I wanted to give up, God would not allow me. I was struggling.

As time went by, I realized I could do this. One evening, Judas called crying and said his nephew passed away. He wanted me to come to support him. At the end of the day, we were still family, so I was willing to support him in any way I could. He came to get me and the kids for the funeral. I could see that the family was really grieving, so I was on my best behavior. We made it through without hurting each other in any way. I felt at peace with my decision to leave. He would check on the kids every day and here and there he would express that he wanted this marriage. So much has happened that I just didn't know if I could ever trust him. Every time I tried to make this work, I got hurt. It was at my expense. Would he ever stop? My guess was no.

I just happened to come across his tablet that he left at the house. I told my daughter that she could use it for school. I wanted to check it first to make sure there weren't any inappropriate things on it. Well, Judas still hadn't been faithful after asking for his family back. He was now entertaining a young lady who was like family to him. I can see they were sending each other pictures and videos. He even told her that she had the body of a goddess. That was crazy to me because we hadn't always been intimate throughout the marriage, even telling the counselor that he wasn't intimate to punish me. What did I do to be treated this way? He was obviously attracted to her. I had never heard him talk like that. There was another side of him I didn't know about. When comforting him, of course, he tried to lie, but I told him no need to lie. I had proof so he should stop. Imagine how many more women he was involved with right under my nose.

The crazy thing is he would tell me he was going with her to different places so that she could show him around. She was like family to him, so I didn't think anything inappropriate was going on. This just gave me more strength. God was showing me why I shouldn't go back. So, I didn't.

I kept pushing to make it on my own even more. I had my bad days when I wanted to run back because he was all I knew for so many years. This was very scary for me. But that was the trick of the enemy.

I ran into my room hearing my phone ring. I answered and it was Judas pouring his little heart out. "I don't want to lose you, I want my marriage. I'm going to make some changes. I'm sorry for everything I put you through. I'm not expecting you to just take me back but to open your heart." Of course, I had an awe moment, and for sure, it was a moment. My birthday was rolling back around. I was unsure of what I wanted to do. On the day of my birthday, I received edible arrangements and beautiful flowers from Judas. I was so confused. I read the card and it said: "Happy birthday, I love you now and always, enjoy your special day." Even though we had been going through rough times, he was still trying to show up but his trying isn't enough at this point.

The next morning my daughter asked me for the charger for the tablet and I couldn't find it anywhere. I was looking all over the house. I ran across it in his drawer in my room, so I plugged it up so she could have it for school that day. As soon as we logged in, his email popped up. I saw edible arrangements. I clicked on the email to see how much he had paid for it because I felt it was a waste of money. I didn't even see my name. I saw Sharea's name and phone number. I put it to good use.

I began talking to myself. "This man just told me he wanted his family back; he's a liar." I had to get to the bottom of things. I decided to call to find out what was going on. I wasn't getting the truth from him. As soon as I dialed the number, she picked up.

She said, "Hello?"

"So, I see you're still sleeping with my husband. I didn't call to fight, I just want to let you know you can have him. I left him. You never have to be second again." What she told me, I wasn't ready for.

"Let me explain something to you. We kept in touch everywhere you guys went. I saw you at the navy ball. I was stationed in North Carolina with you guys; as a matter of fact, he told me the reason he picked you was because you got pregnant with your daughter. He never wanted you, and he couldn't stand you. I was the one he wanted to be with. I received not one edible arrangement but two and flowers. Oh, he didn't tell you that I gave him money to go to pay his last respects to his nephew?"

I replied, "Well, he took his family with your money, so thank you." It was the truth, but I was being petty because I was hurt. "So, you two have been fooling around the entire time we've been married?" I asked.

"On and off for some years. He often asked me, 'How do you think things would have been if we had gotten married?'"

"Okay, like I said, now you guys can run off into the sunset. I'm done with him. He's a liar and the truth isn't in him," I told her.

She responded, "I know he's a big liar and now I'm in a wonderful relationship. I don't want him." We hung up to never speak again. I was so angry that I was breaking things in my house because I couldn't get at him. This woke me up. Eventually, I spoke to him and told him he was a piece of garbage. I didn't want anything to do with him. He came back stating that after she told me all of that, she sent him pictures of herself. Good, you can have each other.

He would come and see the kids but we had nothing going on. That didn't stop Judas from trying but I was done.

Judas came to visit the kids. It was a Friday morning so we dropped the kids off and went to get some breakfast. On my way there, my friend Jamie called. We haven't spoken in a while and we tried to catch up a little, but I didn't want to be rude to Judas. The call lasted about ten minutes. I could tell that Judas was bothered but I didn't pay him any attention because we were no longer together.

Judas said, "Jamie calls and you have a lot to say, but you're lost for words when it comes to me." We began to go back and forth after a while. I got quiet once I saw we were not getting anywhere. As soon as I turned the key to get back into the house, he attacked me, and I was fighting back. At one point my finger went into his mouth from the commotion, and he decided to bite me. I screamed and ran to the kitchen to use the first thing I could find. I saw a screwdriver and threw it at him. He was in shock. It missed his face, hitting the glass table in the living room, and shattering the glass. I called his mother instead of the police to tell him to leave my apartment. That was the last time Judas stayed in our home.

I knew everything that was happening, I was lying to myself, knowing I couldn't trust him or myself. I betrayed myself and sacrificed my happiness just to say I have this, and this was what people called marriage but behind closed doors, it's a war. A spiritual warfare, a battle of the mind. While having women telling me he was never mine. I'm woke now, never going back, back to a place where I will never find peace because the Brooklyn he met is now deceased.

CHAPTER THIRTEEN

I Know The Truth,
No More Living His Lies

No more lies to be told. I knew the truth, and I was finally okay with the reality I had to face. There was a knock at the door, and I was served with divorce papers during the pandemic. Judas had a plan for me but God had one for him. I was hustling to take care of my kids while Judas tried so hard to discredit my name and bring me hardship. He introduced my kids to women he was dealing with and even told other women lies about me but I kept my strength. I had my good days and bad. I got to see who Judas truly was. Who he was and I was willing to stay away. I had to block him from my phone and social media, so I could find my peace. I found myself, I'm worthy of true love. It wasn't me or my weight. The truth is, he was dealing with demons within. I am free of the hurt and pain. Never love someone more than you love yourself... it's not worth it. With everything I've been through, I'm wiser and stronger.

So I want to thank him. God was able to shape and mold me into the woman I am today. I'm helping women like myself to put their lives back together. If you don't love yourself, who will? Love starts with you. I have always been an investor and I only want to attract those who are willing to invest. Making us equally yoked. Remember you matter. Your self-love coach.

God showed me his truth from the very beginning. I was busy lying to myself. Thinking I was winning. Wanting something Judas couldn't provide. Setting aside my needs, instead of falling to my knees. I paid for it all. No more living his lies because I know the truth. I'm worthy and beautifully made. Not knowing this made me stay. Now I'm the author of this new book. I'm in control of this new look at life.

In remembrance of Yeseen
Mommy, love you.

About the Author

Tishana also known as Brooklyn was born and raised in Brooklyn, New York. Her parents came from Panama in search of the American dream to provide for her and her siblings. They always told her that education was very important. Wanting the best for her they put her in one of the top schools in Brooklyn. She attended Bishop Loughlin Memorial High School. At the age of 19 years old, she became a salon owner. This is where she began to counsel women behind the chair. Once Brooklyn became a wife to a military spouse and a mother, she put her career on hold. She understood that her spouse's career was very demanding and her children needed her more. 37 years of age was a turning point for Brooklyn. Life as she knew it changed. She was now separated from her husband and on her own with two kids. Georgia became her state of residency. This was a fresh new start for her and the kids. She made the best of her situation and overcame the storms that came her way. Before you knew it Brooklyn opened a salon, started a fashion line business and took her life experience, and became a life coach.

https://www.linkedin.com/in/tishana-eason-92912761/
https://www.instagram.com/coachbrooklynselfhealing/
www.brooklynbeautybarga.com